WINTER FESTIVALS

Mike Rosen

Wayland

Seasonal Festivals

Autumn Festivals
Winter Festivals
Spring Festivals
Summer Festivals

Editor: Tracey Smith and Geraldine Purcell
Designer: Ross George

Cover: Chinese New Year Lion and Dragon Dance,
Hong Kong.

First published in 1990 by
Wayland (Publishers) Limited
61 Western Road, Hove
East Sussex, BN3 1JD, England

British Library Cataloguing in Publication Data
Rosen, Mike 1959–
  Winter festivals.
  1. Festivals
  I. Title II. Series
  394.2

ISBN 1–85210–877–0

© Copyright 1990 Wayland (Publishers) Limited

2nd impression 1991

Typeset by Rachel Gibbs, Wayland
Printed by G. Canale C.S.p.A., Turin
Bound by Casterman S.A., Belgium.

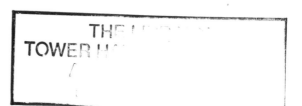

Contents

Winter

Winter climates vary greatly in different parts of the world. The temperate zones are those areas of the world with a moderate temperature, lying between the tropics and the polar regions. Winter in these areas can be very hard. In woods and forests, the bare branches of trees contrast with leafy evergreens. Some animals hibernate until the warmth of spring. For others, food is in short supply as fields are empty and frozen. Throughout the winter there may be heavy frosts which last all day, the ground may be frozen hard, and snow may fall, collecting around parked cars, walls and hedgerows in deep drifts.

In the temperate zones the coldest winter weather arrives several weeks after the winter solstice. This solstice, which occurs around the middle of December in the northern hemisphere, can be thought of as being midwinter day.

Left **These children in Finland are making candles by dipping lengths of wick into melted wax. On Christmas Eve the candles will be placed at the graves of family and friends.**

4

When it is cold, people dress in warm clothes. In some countries children enjoy winter sports such as skiing, tobogganing and ice skating. Getting to school or work can be dangerous when the roads are icy or blocked with snow. Farmers move their animals from winter pastures and shelter them in farm buildings to keep them warm and safe. Food festivals and New Year celebrations are popular events, as they remind people that winter will not last forever.

Some parts of the world have a very different type of winter. Children who live in tropical countries will probably never see ice or snow. But their winter weather may include strong winds, such as the Harmattan, which blows through parts of Africa in January and February.

At the North and South Poles the weather is always extremely cold. In winter, the sun barely rises above the horizon and the only light is provided by the moon.

Above **Many farm animals are moved to specially chosen winter pastures in order to protect them from the worst of the winter weather. However, animals such as sheep can be quite hardy. Their warm winter coats help them to endure harsh winter conditions.**

Festivals of the Solstice

Left Many ancient customs survive in strange ways. The peoples of northern Europe burnt a large log at their Yule solstice celebrations. This cake has been made in the shape of a Yule log for a Christmas party in France.

The shortest day of the year occurs at the winter solstice. For ancient peoples, whose agricultural life depended on the sun, it was a day to celebrate. They knew that after the solstice the sun would grow stronger and the hours of daylight would increase. There was a fear that this yearly change might not happen, and the sun would continue to weaken until it finally disappeared. So people held ceremonies in honour of the sun, to welcome its returning strength and help it grow.

Traditional solstice festivals from northern Europe included bonfire celebrations and torchlit processions. During the festival of Yule, held in Scandinavia, Germany and Britain, a large log – sometimes a whole tree trunk – would be kept burning for three days while people feasted and celebrated. After the third day, some of the ash from the Yule log would be collected to be kept as a source of good luck for the next year.

The people of northern Europe believed that the spirits of the dead joined them for the celebrations at Yule. In China too, the solstice is still a time to remember the dead. At the winter solstice, the spirits of dead ancestors are invited to eat with the living family at a special feast. Places are left empty at the table and portions of food are served for the spirits to eat if they want to. Another Chinese custom is to make clothes and money from paper. It is believed that when these are burnt they will be taken by the wind to the spirits and will make the family's dead ancestors wealthy.

Left In Finland lighted candles are placed at family graves on Christmas Eve. This custom may have grown from the ancient belief of northern Europeans that the spirits of dead people visited their families at the winter solstice.

Christmas

On 25 December many Christians all over the world celebrate the birth of Christ. At that time in northern and central Europe, Canada, and much of the USA and USSR, it is deepest winter. The southern hemisphere is made up of those lands that are south of the equator, such as Australia, southern Africa and South America. Christmas in these countries falls in midsummer when, on 25 December, the sun is at its furthest point south. When the weather is hot and the sun is shining on Christmas day, it is difficult to believe that Christmas began in the northern hemisphere as a winter solstice festival.

The origins of Christmas lie in history. In the Middle Ages, Christianity became the official religion of most European rulers, and, over the centuries, was spread around the world by European soldiers, traders, and missionaries. There are now Christians in most countries of the world but the celebration

Below In Sweden the festival of St Lucia is held on 13 December. The girl who has been chosen as the Lucia queen leads a procession through the streets from house to house. All the girls in the procession are dressed in long white robes and carry candles. The Lucia queen wears a crown of candles on her head.

of Christmas began in the northern hemisphere – where the winter solstice is 21 December.

Christianity became the official religion of the Roman Empire in the fourth century. The Romans already worshipped many gods and goddesses, each of whom had their own festival. At the winter solstice the Romans held a festival called Saturnalia. It was a very popular festival, with feasting and celebrations lasting for several days. The first Christians chose to celebrate the birth of Christ at that time. When the Roman Empire became Christian, Christmas replaced Saturnalia as the winter solstice festival, but many of the traditions of Saturnalia were continued in the Christmas celebrations. As Christianity spread to other lands, its main festival adopted traditions from the solstice celebrations of those countries. They still form part of some modern Christmas celebrations.

Above **The festival of Saturnalia was one of the main celebrations in the Roman year. Many of the ways in which the Romans celebrated have become traditional parts of the Christian festival of Christmas.**

Christmas Traditions

The ways of celebrating Christmas have changed little since it replaced Saturnalia. From Saturnalia came the traditions of feasting, giving parties and decorating homes with evergreen plants such as holly and ivy – a reminder that even at midwinter the powers of nature survived. When Christianity came to northern Europe, the missionaries found that the Celts and other local tribes also honoured the evergreens at the winter solstice. Mistletoe was a sacred plant to the Druids of Britain and, although it was never used as an official part of Christian celebrations, at Christmas many British people still pin a sprig of mistletoe over a fireplace or at the entrance to the home.

Left The festival of Christmas is now celebrated in countries far from the original home of Christianity in the Middle East. These lights have been set up on a building in Hong Kong.

Left **To many children, looking forward to a visit from Santa Claus is the most exciting part of Christmas. Every year thousands of letters are posted to Greenland, the traditional home of Santa Claus, by children all over the world.**

Other Christmas customs have come from northern Europe. Some ancient peoples believed that at the winter solstice the god Odin visited earth to reward good and punish evil. As Christianity spread, St Nicholas replaced Odin in the solstice legends, bringing gifts at Christmas to good children. In the Netherlands there is still a festival of St Nicholas on 6 December. The name Santa Claus has developed from the Dutch name for St Nicholas – Sinterklaas.

At Christmas, families come together to eat on Christmas Day. Many Christians go to church on Christmas Eve for a special ceremony at midnight to welcome the day when Christ was born. Relatives and friends give presents, and on Christmas morning, children wake eagerly to see if Santa Claus has left them a special gift.

In countries with warm climates, Christmas is also a time for public celebrations. In Australia there are huge parades with marching bands. In Bombay and Goa in India there are midnight services held outdoors.

Winter Solstice in Peru

The people of Peru in South America follow Christian beliefs that were introduced in the sixteenth century by their Spanish and Portuguese conquerors. Despite this, some festivals are still held which celebrate the beliefs of the ancient peoples who lived there before the Europeans arrived.

One Inca festival was held on 24 June, three days after the winter solstice in the southern hemisphere, in honour of the sun-god, Inti. An important part of the festival was watching the sun rise at dawn. Some Peruvians still watch the sun rise on this date, at the ancient Inca fortress of Sacsahuaman, near the town of Cuzco. As this ceremony is held to remind Peruvians of Inca traditions, Inca clothes are

Above **These Peruvians are wearing the traditional robes used by religious leaders. The hand-woven cloth and embroidery are typical of these clothes.**

worn. These wool or cotton costumes (tunics for the men and long dresses for the women) are dyed in rich colours such as turquoise, red, yellow, purple, white and pink. They are decorated with patterns of stripes, squares, triangles, circles and other geometric shapes.

In Inca times, there were ceremonial rituals and sacrifices of animals to the sun-god, before a celebration feast. The details of these ceremonies have been forgotten since the time of the Spanish invasion. The Spanish changed the date of the Inca winter solstice festival to that of the Catholic holy day of Corpus Christi (between mid-May and mid-June). In parts of Peru, Bolivia, and Chile, Corpus Christi is still celebrated with a mixture of processions, feasts and ceremonies taken from both Inca and Catholic traditions.

Below **The festival procession for Inti Raimi. This celebration takes place at the ruined Inca fort of Sacsahuaman in June, which in the southern hemisphere is midwinter.**

Pongal

Left Before the Pongal festival begins, families clean their homes carefully. Then the women and children may draw colourful patterns in chalk on the floors and courtyards.

Pongal is a three-day festival held in the state of Tamil Nadu in southern India. Solstice celebrations form only a part of the festival in Tamil Nadu. Pongal also gives thanks for the rainy season and celebrates the January rice harvest.

On the first day of Pongal, gifts are taken to the temples in thanks for the rain which has helped the crops to grow. A traditional Pongal gift is a clay statue of a horse. Often painted in bright colours, these statues can be almost a metre tall. Other gifts given to the temple may be food, oil and incense for ceremonies, or money to pay for repairs.

The next day is the solstice celebration. Again gifts are taken to the temple – this time in honour of the sun's returning strength. On this day, traditional gifts are fresh sweets made from fruits and the new rice of the recent harvest. After the ceremony the sweets will be shared out among the people who have offered them.

The final day of Pongal is dedicated to the cattle. Cattle have traditionally pulled the ploughs through the rice fields of India and, on this day, their owners thank them for their help with the harvest. The animals are washed and their horns may be painted and decorated with flowers. In the evening of the third day the festival ends with a procession of cattle, a large feast, and a competition when men try to snatch bundles of money from between the horns of a fierce bull.

Below **Cattle are holy animals to many Indians. At the Pongal festival each animal is bathed before a garland is placed around its neck and its horns are painted in bright colours.**

Festivals of New Year

For much of the world 1 January is celebrated as New Year's Day. Originally, this was the date of the Roman New Year. Although it occurs in the middle of summer in the southern hemisphere, like Christmas, this is truly a winter festival.

On New Year's Eve, 31 December, many people hold parties which last until late into the night. It is traditional to greet the new year at midnight on 31 December and celebrate the first minutes of the year in the company of friends and relatives. People may dance and sing together and drink a toast to the year ahead.

Below **As part of the New Year celebrations in the USSR, people gather by candlelight in the main square of their town. These people are celebrating the beginning of the 1990s in Red Square, Moscow.**

After the celebrations, it is time to make new year resolutions – these are a list of decisions about how to live in the coming year. Often people resolve to be honest and more generous in their relationships with others, or they may set themselves new aims to achieve at work or in their leisure activities. New Year's Day is the first day they must put these resolutions into practice.

In Scotland, New Year's Eve is called Hogmanay. It is celebrated with bonfires and feasts. At midnight a song called *Auld Lang Syne* is sung. This tells people to remember the past and look forward to the future. It is also believed that the first person to enter your home after midnight can bring you good luck. If this person carries the traditional gifts of bread, coal, and money then the family will not be poor, cold, or hungry in the coming year.

Above **Lights and bonfires are an important part of many festivals held in winter. These lanterns have been laid on the hillside outside the Japanese city of Kyoto as part of the New Year celebrations.**

17

Chinese New Year

Left At the Chinese New Year celebrations in London, people fill the streets to watch the spectacular processions. Similar celebrations are held in Hong Kong and San Francisco, but in China itself this festival is thought of as a quiet family celebration and there are no huge public processions.

Traditionally, the Chinese have used a lunar calendar, and because of this, their New Year does not start on 1 January. The Ancient Chinese fixed the date of their New Year according to the position of the sun. The first day of the traditional Chinese year varies from year to year and occurs sometime between 21 January and 20 February.

Chinese New Year is celebrated most spectacularly by those Chinese people who live outside China. Some of the largest and best-known celebrations take place in Hong Kong, the USA and Britain. For people in these countries, Chinese New Year is both a family event and a public celebration.

Left **Chinese New Year processions can be very spectacular. Lettuce and money are traditional gifts for dancers to collect as they move from house to house.**

In China, the beginning of a new year is celebrated more quietly, with few public ceremonies. For most of the twentieth century, the government of China has wanted the Chinese people to stop celebrating traditional customs and beliefs and has discouraged public celebration of the old festivals. This attitude has led to most traditional festivals being thought of as private family celebrations.

Although China's government now uses the Gregorian calendar, in which the year begins on 1 January, the traditional date set by the lunar calendar has continued to be used for the celebration of Chinese New Year. It is the festivities in countries far away from China that have helped the celebration of this ancient festival to survive.

Chinese New Year Customs

One week before the New Year begins, the family gathers for a ceremony in honour of the god of the kitchen. This god is believed to journey to the Emperor of Heaven and report on the family's thoughts and actions over the past year. A picture of the kitchen-god is burnt. This allows the god to leave the house, but first, the lips are smeared with honey so that only good things about the family will be told. Some families keep statues of the god, whose lips may also be smeared with honey.

On the evening before New Year, the kitchen-god is welcomed back into the home with a feast and fireworks. At New Year people eat only vegetarian meals which contain no meat. This is because each year is named after an animal. One special food is Jiaozi, dumplings made with sweetened flour which

Below **This exciting New Year firework display was held in Hong Kong. Fireworks are a beautiful and important part of the celebration of the Chinese New Year all over the world.**

have money, gifts, or messages of good luck inside. Some of the food is set out for the spirits of dead ancestors to eat, so that they too will have a happy New Year. Children are given gifts of money, and people try to pay back any debts before the new year starts.

On New Year's Day the festival moves into the streets. Usually, an enormous paper dragon, moved by many men inside its body, dances through the streets to the music of drums. Over the doorways of houses and shops hang parcels of money which the dancers collect. This money is used to help the community and good fortune is brought to those whose money is accepted. As evening falls there may be firework displays before people return home to honour their family gods once more.

Above **The most exciting part of a New Year procession is the dance performed by men holding a colourful model of a dragon or lion. The dancers twist the gigantic model in dramatic swooping movements and shake its head, seeming to make the animal come to life.**

Japanese New Year

Japan now uses the Gregorian calendar, which places New Year on 1 January. Many Japanese celebrate this festival in ways which reflect traditional beliefs taken from the Buddhist and Shinto religions.

For Japanese Buddhists, New Year's Eve is an important day. They will think about the good things that happened during the past year, and about the need to continue the struggle against evil. At midnight the temple bells are rung 108 times – this is a sacred number for Buddhists – as part of a ceremony which allows the year to begin, free of evil.

Japanese families who follow the Shinto tradition prepare for New Year with a ritual cleansing of the house on 13 December. As New Year's Day approaches decorations are placed around the house. Small evergreen fir trees remind the family that many things remain constant at a time of change. Straight lengths of bamboo represent the importance of honesty. Above the front door hangs a

Left **The Japanese women here are putting up traditional decorations for their New Year celebrations. These are intended to keep bad luck away during the coming year.**

Left This Japanese trader is dressed in the traditional costume of Ebisu, one of the seven gods of good luck from Japan's ancient religions. Wearing this costume should bring the trader good luck in the new year.

decoration made of paper and rice-straw, which is intended to keep bad luck outside the house and bring good fortune in.

On New Year's Day families exchange gifts, and it is the custom for people to forgive anyone who may have hurt or angered them. Afterwards, traditional foods are eaten. These include a vegetable stew with rice cakes, and foods which are said to bring good fortune, such as black beans for good health or seaweed for happiness. The day after New Year there are processions, and demonstrations by artists and traders showing what they have achieved in the old year. These are believed to bring good fortune for the new year.

Carnival

Carnival celebrations happen in many countries where Christianity is the main religion. These festivities take place just before Lent, which is a period of 40 days before Easter. Lent is traditionally a time of fasting, when Christians do not allow themselves to eat certain foods. The word carnival comes from the Latin words *carnem levare* (which mean 'to take away meat'). As Lent begins on Ash Wednesday, carnival must end at midnight the day before, which is called Shrove Tuesday.

Carnivals usually include processions of decorated floats. In Spain, Portugal, and the Caribbean an important part of carnival is a pageant which includes giant puppets of famous people. Another custom, celebrated

Left **At the Mardi Gras celebrations in New Orleans, people dance in the streets to the music of marching jazz bands. Many people wear costumes that are similar to those worn by men and women in New Orleans at the end of the nineteenth century.**

especially in Italy and France, is a mock battle with flowers. This is a traditional celebration of the arrival of new blooms as winter ends. In the Caribbean, particularly on the island of Trinidad, the beautiful music of steel drum bands and Calypso songs, which may make fun of people and make the audience laugh, are important parts of carnival celebrations.

In France, carnival is known as Mardi Gras (*Fat Tuesday*). Mardi Gras spread from France to the parts of the USA where French people had settled. The Mardi Gras celebrations in New Orleans, USA are the most spectacular. Huge crowds pack the streets to see the procession of decorated floats. Between the floats are groups of costumed dancers, often wearing masks. They perform wild dances to the joyous sound of traditional-jazz bands whose clarinets and cornets blast their melodies over the noise of the crowds.

Above **This car, with its bright colours and decorations of jewellery, is one of many such vehicles which take part in the parades during the Mardi Gras celebrations.**

Carnival in Rio

Carnival was originally a seasonal festival, which celebrated the end of winter and the beginning of spring, but in Rio it occurs at the end of summer. This is because Rio is in the southern hemisphere and enjoys summer while the northern hemisphere has winter.

Planning for carnival starts early. The people of Rio get together in groups called Samba schools, hoping that their school will win the prize awarded for the best display. Although many parts of Rio are very poor, everyone wants to help their school and there always seems to be money for the carnival planners to spend. Fantastic costumes use many metres of bright materials, as the designers compete to have the most exciting image. The floats may be 10 m tall and just

Above **One of the enormous and spectacular floats designed each year for the Rio carnival. As soon as each carnival ends people start planning for the next one.**

as long, with complicated decorations of carved wood or metal painted gold or silver. On the float rides the queen of the school, who has been chosen for the year. Her costume is often so elaborate that it seems to be part of the float and she hardly dares move in case the effect is spoiled.

The music of carnival in Rio is Samba. Choruses of horns combine with guitars and steel bands to produce exciting rhythms. Dancers move together in carefully planned dances, mixing individual skills with careful teamwork. The dancing continues at street parties all over Rio until late in the night – especially in the area whose Samba school has won the prize.

Below **Dancers like these practise their complicated dances many times before the carnival parade. They get together with other people to form a school of dancers. A prize is given for the best group.**

Snow Festivals

In many countries, snow is a normal part of winter. When the snow lies thickly on the ground children and adults play winter games, sledging or throwing snowballs at each other. Another custom is to shape a huge mound of snow to look like a person or sometimes an animal. There is a festival in Quebec in Canada during which people carve statues out of ice. Similar festivals are held in Japan, especially in towns in the north, such as Sapporo, where huge and beautiful sculptures are made from snow.

Left **Ice carvings are a popular part of many winter festivals. Ice statues, such as this one in Austria, can be made in any country where the weather is cold enough to keep the ice frozen.**

Children in Japan celebrate a snow festival at the beginning of February. In parts of northern Japan, such as the area around Akita, there is still thick snow at this time of year. Children build themselves igloos. These are dome shaped huts, which are built with carefully made blocks of snow. There is a small shrine inside each igloo in honour of the spirits which bring water. The candles on the shrine light the igloo so well that, from a distance, it seems to glow in the dark. On one night of the festival the children are allowed to stay awake in the igloos until daylight comes. Through the night they are visited by adult friends and relatives. The children give each adult a drink and a cake of toasted rice. In return the adults give the children some money.

Above **This picture shows how snow sculptures and statues can be decorated with lights at night. These huge models were photographed during the winter ice festival in Quebec, Canada.**

Glossary

Evergreen A word used to describe plants which continue to bear leaves, fruit, or berries through the winter.

Gregorian Calendar This calendar was named after Pope Gregory XIII, who introduced its use in 1582. The Gregorian calendar adds one day to the length of the year once every four years. This brought the calendar into line with the solar year which is actually 365¼ days long.

Hemisphere Half of the Earth's sphere.

Hibernate To spend the winter in a state similar to a deep sleep. Hibernation helps many mammals to survive the winter.

Lunar Calendar A calendar which is organized according to the waxing and waning of the moon.

Missionaries People who are sent out, often to another country, on religious work.

Pageant A colourful public show or parade, where people may dress as famous or historical figures.

Sometimes a pageant may tell the story of famous events in history. Puppets or masks can be used in a pageant.

Pastures Land suitable for grazing sheep or cattle.

Solstice The two times of year when there is the greatest difference between the hours of daylight and the hours of night-time. At the winter solstice the day is shortest; at the summer solstice the day is longest.

Temperate Zones The areas of the earth's surface between the tropical and polar zones in each hemisphere. It is in these temperate zones that the four seasons of autumn, winter, spring and summer are most different.

Tropical Zones The areas of the earth's surface on either side of the Equator between the Tropic of Cancer and the Tropic of Capricorn. The two tropics mark the furthest points north and south at which the sun is overhead during the summer solstice in each hemisphere.

Books to Read

After reading this book, you might want to find out more about some of the festivals mentioned in it. These books will help you. Ask the librarian at your local library to help you to find them.

Buddhist Festivals, by J Snelling (Wayland, 1983)

Carnival, by J Mayled (Wayland, 1987)

Christmas, by A Blackwood (Wayland, 1987)

Festivals and Celebrations, by R Purton (Basil Blackwell, 1983)

Festivals and Customs, by N J Bull (Arnold Wheaton, 1979)

Festivals Around the World, by P Steele (Macmillan, 1983)

Hindu Festivals, by S Mitter (Wayland, 1985)

India Celebrates, by J W Watson (Garrard, Illinois, 1974)

Investigating Places of Worship, by C B Green (Arnold Wheaton, 1989)

Jewish Festivals, by R Turner (Wayland, 1985)

Projects for Christmas, by M A Green (Wayland, 1989)

Projects for Winter, by C McInnes (Wayland, 1989)

Sikh Festivals, by S S Kapoor (Wayland, 1985)

Winter, by R Whitlock (Wayland, 1987)

Picture Acknowledgements

The publishers would like to thank the following for allowing their pictures to be reproduced in this book:

Barnaby's Picture Library 10, 19, 21; Cephas 28; Eye Ubiquitous 17, 23; Hutchison Library 12, 13, 14, 15, 16; The Mansell Collection 9; Photri 4, 6, 7, 11, 24, 29; Tony Stone Worldwide 5, 18, 20, 26, 27; and Topham 8, 22, 25. All artwork is by Maggie Downer. Cover Spectrum Colour Library/Jean Kugler.

Index